W9-CCX-221

HOW TO BE
More Tree

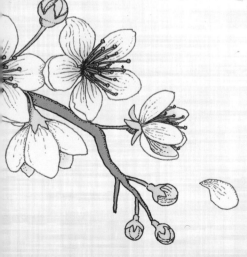

HOW TO BE
More Tree

Essential Life Lessons for
Perennial Happiness

ILLUSTRATED BY
ANNIE DAVIDSON

WRITTEN BY LIZ MARVIN

Clarkson Potter/Publishers
New York

Copyright © 2019 by
Michael O'Mara Books Ltd.

All rights reserved.
Published in the United States by
Clarkson Potter/Publishers, an imprint
of Random House, a division of Penguin
Random House LLC, New York.
clarksonpotter.com

CLARKSON POTTER is a trademark and
POTTER with colophon is a registered
trademark of Penguin Random House LLC.

Originally published in slightly different form
in Great Britain by LOM Art, an imprint of
Michael O'Mara Books Ltd., London, 2019.

ISBN 978-0-593-13916-5
Ebook ISBN 978-0-593-13917-2

Printed in China

Cover illustration by Annie Davidson
Cover design by Jan Derevjanik
Book design by Claire Cater

10 9 8 7 6 5 4 3 2

First American Edition

Introduction

Trees are truly amazing. Sure, they change carbon dioxide into oxygen, which is pretty important if you like breathing, but did you know they also build networks with other trees, can take action when they are being threatened, and have all sorts of clever ways to carry on growing even when they are knocked flat? Trees have been around for nearly 400 million years – a good amount of time to accumulate some serious wisdom – and they've become masters at adapting, surviving, and thriving.

In our complex and often confusing human existence, it's not always easy to keep a cool head and a happy heart. If something is getting under your bark, or you're suffering from a few snapped branches, or you just need reminding to enjoy the feeling of the sun on your foliage, we hope you'll find the inspiration in these pages to help deal with life's bumps and bruises. So sit back, let the wind gently rustle your canopy, and discover how to be more tree.

Beginnings are always small

JAPANESE MAPLE

When you have big dreams it's natural to want to make them happen straightaway. But, as a wise person once said, patience isn't in the waiting, it's in how you deal with having to wait. And Japanese maples have this all worked out. These little trees grow in the mountains, where the pace of life is slow, winters can be hard, and it's not a great idea to overstretch yourself. In time, though, they grow up to have stunning autumn foliage and an effortlessly elegant shape.

Patience is a virtue

YEW

Patience, planning, and taking time to reflect on our experiences is an important part of figuring out where we're going. The yew is the wise old grandmother of trees – it is traditionally associated with magic, and is thought to be able to live for up to 2,000 years. It's hard to tell exactly, though, because yews are coy about their age – older trees are hollow, so we can't count the rings. Part of the secret to their longevity is that they are slow growing but develop extensive root systems in which they can store nutrients in case the tree is ever damaged. So, like the yew, go slow, and feel free to be slightly mysterious.

Draw strength from others

ASPEN

Making the effort to connect with those around us
can bring powerful results. The aspen knows there's
no prize for acting like a tough guy who doesn't need
anyone – in fact, belonging to something bigger than
themselves is key to their strength. Each straight-trunked
tree may look like a tall and proud individual, but under
the surface it is part of a single organism, connected
by their root system to all the other trees in the stand.
If one tree is closer to water or important nutrients,
it can share the goodies with the rest of the gang.

Ask for help when you need it

ELM

The elm is not embarrassed to ask for help when it finds itself in a tricky situation. If it comes under attack from caterpillars, it releases pheromones to attract parasitic wasps, who then lay their eggs inside the caterpillars and neutralize the threat. We often think that self-reliance is the key to success, but the elm knows that you don't need to try to handle everything yourself. Sometimes you just have to call in the wasps.

Adapt to your environment

AMERICAN BEECH

Ever let life's little niggles get under your bark? The ancestors of the American beech did. This tree started out in the tropics, where annoying little plants called epiphytes would try to grow in the cracks of its trunk. So the American beech developed a lovely smooth bark and the epiphytes were out of luck. Consciously work on developing an even, calm exterior and you'll find your personal epiphytes will roll right off.

Be authentic

HORNBEAM

It's sometimes difficult to be wholly ourselves in every situation; there's often a temptation to change who we are to please the crowd. Learning to be authentic means accepting and enjoying the bark we're in. Trees don't waste chlorophyll trying to be something they're not. They focus on their own growth without worrying about what everyone else is up to. Take the humble hornbeam: It doesn't grow particularly tall, or produce fancy flowers or delicious fruit. But it's been around for many thousands of years, growing strong and solid, without expecting a round of applause.

Always have a Plan B

BLACKTHORN

You never know when there might be a herd of hungry goats or a moth infestation just around the corner, right? So it's always good to have a backup plan. Even trees like the blackthorn – which, if you've ever been caught by one while collecting sloes for gin, you'll know are very much All About Thorns – have a second line of defense in case implanting a big barb into someone's skin doesn't work. If a branch is snipped, they release "wound hormones" called jasmonates – a master regulator that then mobilizes all the other chemical defenses and repair systems the tree has at its disposal.

Love where you live

WILLOW

It's hard to thrive if you don't take care of your immediate environment. The willow doesn't put up with a messy riverbank or a grubby river – it shores up crumbly soil with its root system and turns pollutants in the water into fertilizing nitrates. Self-care can start with something as simple as lovely new bed linen, a special lunch, or a stabilized riverbank.

Bask in the sun

MOUNTAIN HEMLOCK

Serotonin is nicknamed "the happy chemical" because higher levels in our brains correlate with feeling positive and calm. Scientists are not sure why, but they think that our brains release more serotonin when we're out in the sunshine. There's certainly no doubt that spending time outdoors is vital for our well-being. Trees can't survive without sunlight, and those like the coniferous mountain hemlock need lots of it. So when you're next thinking of staying inside on a sunny day, consider this: If the mountain hemlock had legs, it would use them to take it to the sunniest spot it could find, every time.

Find your happy place

ALDER

We all need different things in order to thrive – the trick is to find what works for you. Some of us bask in full sun; others love the challenging conditions of a windy mountaintop. Most of us wouldn't feel like our best selves if we stood around in a swamp all day, but this suits the alder down to the ground. Its secret is the bacteria that live in its root nodules. The tree supplies the sugars the bacteria need; the bacteria supply nutrients missing from the waterlogged soil. The result is that the alder flourishes where other trees can't.

Attend to your core

BLACK WALNUT

Focus on building your inner strength and you'll have
a solid trunk to support you through the stresses of
everyday life. Trees are masters of this – after all, their
trunk has to support all the weight of their branches
and foliage on the windiest of days. The center of the
trunk is called the heartwood, and the black walnut in
particular has some impressive inner steel. It is admired
for its beauty and its strength, and its heartwood is so
tough it can withstand huge force without fragmenting.

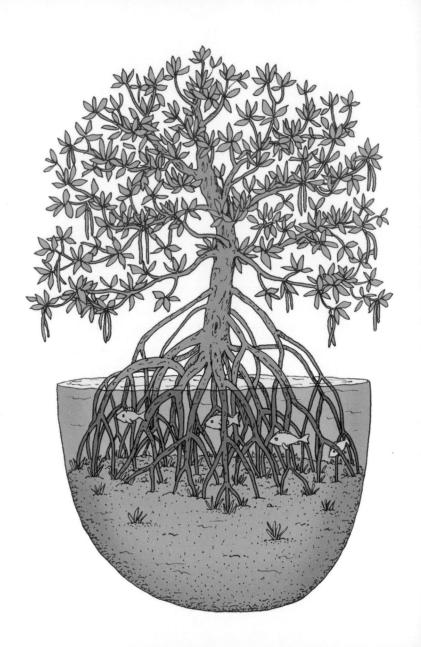

Plan for the future

MANGROVE

Life can often feel like a struggle, and it's easy to get caught up in dealing with the day-to-day. Although thoughts of the future can be overwhelming, it really does pay to plan ahead. Mangroves have developed some amazing adaptations so they can live in salty water, even finding a clever way to use the water to spread future generations of trees. Instead of seeds, mangroves produce little seedlings called propagules that grow from the parent plant until they are big enough to float away on the current and take root in their own spot.

Look on the bright side

CHESTNUT

Learning to live in the moment means that when the good times come around, you're open to making the most of them. Every May, chestnuts grow beautiful blossoms known as candles. The smell attracts lots of insects, and everyone is invited to a big old pollen party. This feel-good vibe brings rewards in the shape of pollination, and come the autumn its boughs hang heavy with lots of glossy conkers. Sure, one day it will be winter again, but while the sun shines, party and grow flowers.

'Don't be afraid to branch out

LONDON PLANE

Step outside your comfort zone and you'll be
surprised what you can achieve. The London plane
isn't an indigenous urbanite – it's the offspring of
the Asian plane and American sycamore – but it has
embraced its new environment and adapted perfectly
to city living. Its bark peels, meaning it can shed soot
and other pollutants, and it deals stoically with having
its roots rudely tarmacked over by city planners.

Get plenty of rest

SILVER FIR

"Make hay while the sun shines," they say. And when it doesn't? Put down your rake and take a load off. Conifers like the silver fir are pros at knowing when to take it easy. These guys keep their needles all year, unlike their broadleaf friends, so they can photosynthesize a little bit on sunny days in the winter. But they still slow right down at this time of year and focus on preventing water loss through their leaves.

Stand tall

BAOBAB

If you ever need a reminder to stand tall and be proud
of what you can do, have a look at the baobab. There's
no polite way of saying it: this tree looks a little … odd.
But it has some awesome skills. The baobab thrives in the
harsh conditions of the African savannah, and while other
trees might have to put up with being nibbled by goats
or even a giraffe or two, the baobab has to contend with
the attentions of thirsty elephants penetrating its soft bark.
It's possibly the only tree that can expand to store water,
and it can live for around 2,000 years. Pretty impressive
for a tree that looks like it's growing upside down.

Be creative

HOLLY

Sometimes the only way to tackle a problem is to come at it sideways, and a bit of lateral thinking can often save the day. In their infinite wisdom, trees know this too, frequently sprouting various types of leaves at different heights to maximize their growth – for example, with fewer or more light-absorbing cells depending on how much sun the leaf gets. The holly takes this one step further, producing more prickles on its lower leaves, where they might get nibbled by passing animals, than on its upper branches.

So, be more holly and don't be afraid to innovate!

Give without expectation

OLIVE

It seems strange in a way that giving something away can bring us joy, but it's true. There's even research that proves it. The olive tree doesn't need to read it, though, as it has known this for thousands of years. You'd think a tree that lives in dry, hot climates in generally poor soil would be most concerned with looking out for itself. And yet it produces fruit with a higher energy content than any other, and can grow them until it's nearly 1,000 years old. This generous tree has been giving away food, medicine, and oil to local humans in unforgiving climes since Neolithic times.

Set your own boundaries

WHITE POPLAR

Allowing yourself to be pushed beyond what you're comfortable with rarely leads to a chilled, happy you. The white poplar is great at lots of things; it can grow in most type of soils, and when there is some newly cleared ground up for grabs, it gets straight in there and shoots up really quickly. But it hates the shade. It needs light to flourish, so that's where it grows. Simple.

Be a good friend

AFRICAN ACACIA

Most trees are much less passive, and much more
sociable, than you would think. The African acacia
knows it's important to look out for your friends.
When some antelope or giraffes stop by for a snack,
the tree pumps out ethylene gas to warn its neighbors,
who can then release tannins into their leaves that
can be poisonous to the hungry herbivores. So,
like the acacia, look after your friends and make
sure you share when scary things happen (although
perhaps try to avoid pumping out too much gas).

When times are tough, take a break

DAHURIAN LARCH

Feeling tired and overwhelmed changes how we see the world. It can make us think a simple shadow is a monster under the bed. The cure? Rest. And being kind to yourself. Take a leaf from the Dahurian larch's … er, leaves. This survival expert grows in the most northerly latitudes. It's learned to get through the long harsh Siberian winters by dropping its needles and laying dormant for a while until friendlier weather arrives.

Life is all about the small wonders

ACAI PALM

Ever noticed how a simple act of kindness can feel like the sun coming out in your day? Small joys – and the sharing of them – is the secret to a happier life. Take the acai palm: It thrives deep in the heart of the complex ecosystem of the Amazon rainforest and makes it its mission to share the love. It attracts over 200 different types of insects with its lovely pollen, and its beautiful and super-nutritious deep purple berries provide dinner for lots of birds, reptiles, and other living things in search of goodness.

Be open to change

BALSAM FIR

There's not much a tree can do about a sudden drought or a nasty cold snap – jetting off on a sunny vacation isn't really an option. Trees have to accept whatever the universe throws at them and adapt to the unexpected, so they've evolved to be pretty flexible. Take the balsam fir, for example. It has worked out a way of surviving at northern latitudes while not dropping its leaves, so it can photosynthesize all year round, and has developed a thick and resinous sap that doesn't freeze. Sure, change can feel uncomfortable, but – for people and for trees – discomfort can often lead to growth.

Don't worry about things you can't control

SÈVE BLEUE

Some things we can change; some things we just have to deal with. For example, if you realized you were living on a whole heap of poisonous metals, you might be a bit perturbed. But the sève bleue has figured out an extremely clever way to cope with the high concentration of nickel in the soil of New Caledonia, where it lives. It uses citric acid to store the nickel in its sap out of harm's way – turning it blue. If you can't change something that's bothering you, finding a way to live with it is far more productive than worrying about it.

Follow your own path

BANYAN

There's usually more than one route to success, and we don't all have to follow the same path. The weird and wonderful banyan is a giant, with the biggest crown of any tree. But it doesn't even start life in the ground. The seed of this enterprising maverick grows as an epiphyte in the cleft of another tree, grabbing water and nutrients from its surroundings. Once it gets going, it lowers some roots to the ground straight from its branches. There really is more than one way to be a tree.

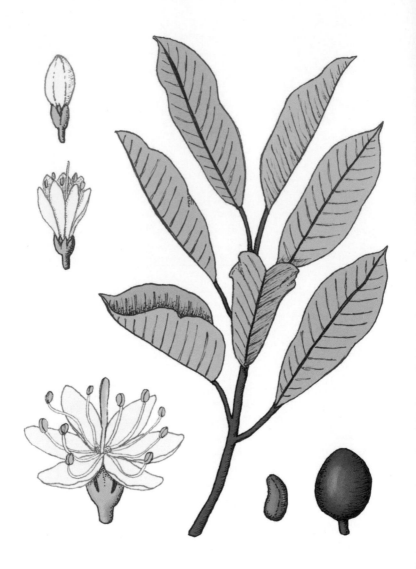

Reach for the sky

GUTTA-PERCHA

The gutta-percha tree is a good reminder that we should never stop learning and growing, or lose sight of our goals. It knows exactly what it wants and goes for it. Earning its stripes in the rainforests of the Malay Peninsula, it has learned that if you want to enjoy the sunshine there, you've got to make a beeline for the forest canopy as fast as you can. So it grows tall and straight, hardly even bothering with branches or leaves below its canopy, until it gets to where it needs to be.

Focus on the positive

GUAREA

Getting knocked down is part of life, and figuring out
how to get back up again is how we learn. Although
if you're a tree, this is easier said than done. When
tropical storms come through Central and South
America, trees like the guarea hang on as best they can,
but sometimes the wind is simply too strong and they
have no choice but to hit the deck. Yet despite finding
itself suddenly horizontal, this tree doesn't give in.
It quickly sprouts new growth along the fallen trunk,
which it feeds with its own food and water until these
"clone" trees are ready to grow roots and go it alone.

It's okay to be different

DRAGON BLOOD

Why fit in when you can stand out? If umbrellas had been used by dinosaurs, they'd have looked like dragon blood trees. Their thick, tall trunks end in a canopy with all the leaves gathered at the top, tightly clustered together to catch water from mist. If you make a small nick in the bark, the tree oozes a deep red resin. In the 1600s, it was dried and imported to Europe, where it was thought to have magical properties, and it's not hard to see why.

The dragon blood tree says: It's cool to be weird.

Learn from your past

CORSICAN PINE

Just like people, trees flourish when they learn from their past experiences. One of the most challenging things for a tree is high winds, which blow even stronger on the kind of exposed slopes the Corsican pine tends to grow on. If you're the tree at the edge of the pine forest, you're going to get hit by the wind even harder. So trees that grow on forest fringes adapt to being buffeted by each winter's winds by changing how they grow, developing a more tapered and stronger trunk.

Live in the moment

YOSHINO CHERRY

Any lucky person who gets to see the amazing blossoms on the Yoshino cherry in real life is sure to be bowled over by the experience. In Japan, families and friends get together to picnic under these beautiful, almost pure-white blooms for the two short weeks they are out. For Buddhists, this is a spiritual experience, which reminds us that beauty, like life, is fleeting, so appreciate it while it's happening and make the most of every moment.

Figure out what's really bothering you

BEECH

We all have times when we feel a bit off-kilter but can't put our finger on exactly why. Spending time on a bit of self-reflection is often the key to getting back on track. Even though trees don't have a lot of options when it comes to solving problems, scientists now think that they have more tools for this at their disposal than previously assumed. For example, the beech can tell if it has been nibbled by deer, and will release tannins to make it taste horrible. If it has simply lost a twig to the wind, however, it will only produce the hormones it needs to seal off that area and heal. So be more beech, and take some time to figure out the cause of your broken twigs.

Accept your limits

GIANT SEQUOIA

We all push ourselves too hard sometimes and don't always appreciate the things within our reach. If this is you, think about the giant sequoia. This amazing tree can grow as tall as a skyscraper, but it still knows when to stop and take stock. Trees use a clever process of evaporation to pump water up to their canopies, where photosynthesis takes place. But the laws of physics dictate that this only works up to about 390 feet. The tallest tree on earth is a giant sequoia called Hyperion that stands at 379 feet. See?

Change with the seasons

CHINESE PISTACHE

One day it's summer and a warm breeze is gently wafting through your branches; the next the nights are drawing in and the threat of frost is in the air. Like trees, we need to develop ways of staying healthy in the most challenging times. Trees lose a lot of water through their leaves, which can't be replaced if the ground is frozen; plus big fluttery foliage would be a nightmare in a winter storm. So broadleaf trees like the Chinese pistache accept they're not going to be photosynthesizing for a while and duly ditch their leaves. No one said it can't do this in style, however. Foliage of the Chinese pistache turns a show-stopping fiery red before it drops, ready for another winter.

Make the most of your community

DOUGLAS FIR

Just like humans, trees benefit from having a support network. Scientists used to wonder why trees like the Douglas fir grow close together, potentially getting in each other's light. It turns out that their roots are connected with the help of fungus in the soil, meaning they can pass nutrients back and forth. When it's important to the rest of the community, the Douglas fir uses this network to nurture the next generation and even keep alive the stump of a tree that has fallen down. And the community isn't just Douglas firs – they're happy to help out their neighbors, even when they are a different tree species.

Love the age you are

COTTONWOOD

We have a tendency to focus on the negatives of aging and overlook the little perks that come with maturity and experience. You won't be surprised to know that trees don't make this mistake. In fact, they *strive* to be older and enjoy it when they get there. The cottonwood is the fastest-growing tree in North America; young trees are ambitious and competitive, shooting up to six feet in one year in their quest to get ahead. This slows as they get older, but this isn't a sign of them giving up. It's just them bulking up, sort of like middle-aged bodybuilders, making them the very best at taking carbon out of the atmosphere.

Nobody's perfect

GINGKO

If we put pressure on ourselves to be brilliant at everything, we just end up feeling stressed and disappointed. The highly accomplished gingko tree is tough as well as beautiful, and fossils show that it has been around for over 200 million years (some at temples in China are thought to be over 1,500 years old). It thrives in polluted cities, even surviving the atomic bomb in Hiroshima. In the autumn, its fan-shaped leaves turn a gorgeous, vibrant yellow. And yet it produces a fruit that smells utterly revolting. You just can't win 'em all!

Let it go

EUROPEAN BOX

Trees get bumps, bruises, and knockbacks, too – and
while they may not be able to move, they know how
to move on! Rather than wasting energy trying to "fix"
a damaged part or fight off an infection, a tree seals off
the area so it doesn't affect the rest of the healthy tissue.
And the European box is the past master – it doesn't
worry about the twigs it's lost. In fact, the redistribution
of the growing hormone auxin means it grows even
bushier and stronger. Which makes it the perfect
hedge. Or topiary, if you're into that kind of thing.

Look after the next generation

SUGAR MAPLE

We've all felt like a small sapling in a big forest at some point. So when you start to get a bit more established, with a little patch of sunlight to call your own, don't forget the little guys coming up behind. Woodland trees like the sugar maple use their underground networks to pump sugars to the younger generation who might be struggling in the shade. So look around. Does anyone in your forest need a bit of help to get them growing?

Be proactive

BALD CYPRESS

Sometimes a bit of time out and self-care is all we need to feel better. But at other times we encounter specific problems that demand practical solutions. Taking the initiative and confronting an issue head-on can be a pretty powerful feeling. The swamp-dwelling bald cypress is a tree that knows how to get things done. Not only has it developed a system to transport air to its roots below the waterline, it's also able to soak up floodwaters, prevent erosion in its watery home, and even help get rid of pollution.

Celebrate your strengths

ASH

We often find it hard to resist comparing ourselves
to others. But trees know that real confidence comes
from valuing what is within. The ash tree produces
some of the strongest wood there is. And it's a speedy
grower. But in the spring, it doesn't rush to be the first
to get its leaves out. While the leaves of the beech and
oak grow densely, meaning that not much can thrive
underneath them, the ash has a much airier canopy,
which allows other plants to sprout in the partial shade
below. So, in short: the ash — strong and confident,
but not that helpful during a sudden rain shower.

Learn to stand on your own

KAURI

Knowing that you have the inner strength to deal with whatever comes your way is important for anyone's confidence. New Zealand's majestic kauri tree has this nailed. These guys can live for over a thousand years, either totally alone or as part of a forest. They are independent with awesome powers of self-sufficiency. Which is lucky really, as their trunks grow so big that it would take seven people holding hands to give them a hug.

Embrace change —
even when it's scary

BANKSIA

The Australian banksia isn't much of a firefighter and, let's face it, its chances of a quick getaway when a bushfire strikes are rather limited. But it knows that even something so destructive can clear the way for new life and new opportunities. The intense heat of the flames actually causes the tree to release its seeds. And as the fire has cleared away all the undergrowth, the plucky little banksia seedlings can now access light and nutrients they couldn't before. Life always returns, and they're determined to be at the front of the line when it does!

Make the most of downtime

OAK

Sleep deprivation is about as useful to trees as it is to people. After a busy summer spent photosynthesizing madly, winter is all about the *zzzzz*. Shedding leaves might seem easy if you've never done it, but it's actually quite an active process. Trees like the oak, whose leaves go brown in the autumn, absorb the nutrients back into their trunks and then grow a barrier of cells between twig and leaf before letting the leaves go. Pretty exhausting stuff. So they put their boughs up and sit out the long, dark nights of winter, contentedly doing very little.

Stand your ground

SCOTS PINE

Take time to get to know yourself and what you really want, and you can be as stoic and confident as the Scots pine (although you still might not want to stand out all day in a Highland wind). This tree has been around for at least 10,000 years, so to be fair, it has had plenty of time for reflection. But it's hard not to be inspired by this tall and powerful native tree that has survived everything the last ten millennia have thrown at it.

Celebrate what you're good at

ROWAN

You don't have to be the biggest or the strongest or the floweriest to thrive. Take the modest little rowan. This slow-growing tree can be found everywhere, from the side of a mountain to a suburban garden. For most of the year you probably wouldn't even notice that it's there. The secret to its success is the bright red berries it grows in the autumn. The birds love them and disperse the rowan's seeds everywhere – in fact, the seeds won't even germinate until they've passed through the gut of a bird.

Learn to weather the storm

HAWTHORN

Queen of country Dolly Parton once said, "Storms make trees take deeper roots," and it's certainly true that trees can adapt to grow in strong winds. While difficult times are inevitable, how we deal with them is up to us. Trees really, really want to grow straight, but tough guys like the hawthorn accept that in exposed places this isn't always possible. The strong prevailing wind damages their growing tips so only the sheltered side grows, making them look lopsided. To keep from falling over, the hawthorn then overbraces its trunk and roots on the opposite side, so it's balanced and much less likely to topple in a storm.

Timing is everything

BEECH

While it is often great to take the initiative, forcing
something before it's ready rarely ends well. The
multitalented beech tree in particular knows this.
Even though its roots have been gearing up for
action all winter and it's looking forward to busting
out some spring foliage, it still bides its time, waiting
until there are at least thirteen hours of light a day.
Trees that jump the gun and leaf as soon as there is a
warm spell often live to regret it. Sort of like when
you put on flip-flops at the first sign of sun and then it
disappears behind the clouds and your toes turn blue.

Don't hold on to what's holding you back

SIERRA PALM

Pride is a funny thing – it can make us feel strong, but it can also be the catalyst for an epic fall from grace. Sometimes we just need to back down to ride out the storm. Take the sierra palm, for example. In tropical places, hurricanes are a way of life, which is dangerous for a tall tree. So, like lots of palms, this tree doesn't hesitate to ditch its leaves in a high wind. Sure, leaves are important and they look nice, but to get through the bad weather the tree needs to present the smallest possible target to the wind. And it can always grow more leaaves once the storm has passed.

Live in harmony

RED CEDAR

One of the big lessons we can learn from trees is how to accept and be at one with all of life's fascinating diversity. The mighty red cedar, native to the Pacific Northwest, seems like a tree that can look after itself, but it still prefers to grow in stands and forests where its roots intertwine with others' to help one another out. Birds help to disperse their seeds and myriad insects and frogs can take shelter in their trunks and branches.

Break out of the everyday

SYCAMORE

Being brave enough to try something new can open the door to personal growth. We know that there are at least 60,000 distinct species of tree. Isn't that amazing? This is because, over many thousands of years, they've adapted to the different situations they've found themselves in. Clever sycamores, for example, learned to turn their seeds into mini helicopters, so the wind carries the large seeds away from the shade of the parent tree without it needing to produce a fruit to be munched by birds and animals. Just remember – someone has to be brave enough to be the first to branch out.

Enjoy the ride

CORK OAK

Life is a journey, and even if everything doesn't always go according to plan, it's important to try to find ways to dance in the rain, rather than waiting for the storm to pass. The cork oak has a very special talent that humans have valued for thousands of years. It has a thick, springy bark that it uses to protect itself from all sorts of things, not least grass fires. And even when local people help themselves to some of it, usually to pop in the top of a nice bottle of wine, the cork oak doesn't mind. Admittedly, it might look a bit naked for a while, but it just carries on regardless and gets busy growing some more. Its resilience and uniqueness make it a king among trees and precious in its native Portugal.

Don't be wasteful

BLACK TUPELO

Trees are great examples of how to make the most of our resources and use what we have as efficiently as possible. For instance, trees such as the black tupelo might look like they are just showing off with their blazing autumn leaf displays, but they are in fact being admirably frugal. Before they chuck away their leaves, deciduous trees make sure to recycle anything that might be useful next year. They reabsorb the green chlorophyll, which leaves behind the yellow and orange colors of chemicals called carotenoids, and the red and purple hues of anthocyanins. Recycling never looked so good.

Offer shelter to others

NEEM

Our relationships with others are important – we all need intimacy and love, and looking after others gives us a sense of purpose and empathy, which in turn can help to reduce stress and anxiety. In its home countries of India and Pakistan, the neem is often found in drought-prone areas where nothing much else will grow, its large canopy providing welcome shade. Its leaves are edible and also contain powerful insect-repelling chemicals, while its nectar is popular with bees. It's not surprising that there's a lot of love for this useful and generous tree.

Put down strong roots

JUNIPER

Trees show us that it's possible to flourish anywhere if
we put down strong enough roots. Take the juniper.
It grows in dry, arid places such as Utah, where it can
look like it has sprouted from solid rock. This very
determined tree has a tap, or central, root that anchors
it to the rock and can grow 40 feet straight down in
search of water. It's so strong that it can push its way
into rock crevices. The juniper also has smaller roots
that spread out sideways so they can quickly slurp
up water from a rain shower before it runs away.

You don't have to be the star of the show

SILVER BIRCH

Taking pride in your work, even when it seems humble, can bring real satisfaction. The silver birch can't really give itself a pat on the back, which is a shame because this tree has been working hard since the last ice age. When a clearing is created, it's the sprightly and stylish silver birch that, partly thanks to the wind dispersing its tiny seeds, goes in first and prepares the ground for the other trees. And then, as its lifecycle is only about eighty years, it pops off and lets the new woodland get on with it, without expecting so much as a thank-you card.

Be careful which way you lean

COOK PINE

"A tree falls the way it leans," says Dr. Seuss, so make sure you're leaning toward the right things in life and relying on the right people. Generally, trees prefer to grow straight; their cells contain little pocket-shaped structures that quite literally tell them which way is up. The tall, slim Cook pine, however, has adopted a more innovative approach to gravity: It likes to lean. Wherever these trees are, they tilt toward the equator, increasing the angle depending on their distance from it. Scientists think that this bold move might be to maximize the sunshine the leaves receive at different latitudes. So, like the Cook pine, try to tilt toward what's good for you.

Be flexible

HAZEL

"Bend so you don't break" is a motto all trees agree with, and one humans can use, too. Trees have to be able to flex so they aren't knocked flat by strong winds, in the same way that we need to adapt when life throws us a curveball. In terms of resilience and flexibility, the hazel is the yogi of trees. It is self-coppicing, which means it sends up new shoots from the base of its trunk every year. These shoots grow into straight and supple rods, which have proved indispensable to humans for thousands of years. "Tough but bendy" is very much the hazel way.

Happiness is a choice

LILAC

As a famous song once instructed, you've got to accentuate
the positive and eliminate the negative. If the lilac had
its own theme tune, it would probably choose this one.
It knows that deciding to focus on the good things is
the first step on the path to feeling happy. This little tree
often finds itself growing in poor soil or in polluted
urban environments, but for two weeks every year it
still flowers its heart out, producing beautiful, fragrant
blooms that attract numerous bees and butterflies.

Save for a rainy day

JARRAH

It's easier to be more mindful in the present if we feel secure about what the future might bring. Knowing we have something to draw on in tough times — whether that's emotionally, practically, or financially — is very reassuring. Similarly, the jarrah hopes that any bushfire to come through its Australian home will pass by quickly, just lightly toasting its trunk. However, if anything more serious happens, it has taken out an insurance policy: Just below the ground, it grows a store of nutrients known as a lignotuber, from which another jarrah can grow should it die. If the damage is less serious, it can also sprout new buds from its trunk. Either way, it's got something in the bank.

Get in touch with your spiritual side

PEEPAL

There are almost as many interpretations of "spirituality" as there are types of tree, but whatever it means to you, it starts with finding a way to connect to an inner voice that can lead you toward a sense of peace. You could say that the peepal, or bodhi tree, is one of the most spiritual of trees. In the sixth century BC, Buddha reached enlightenment while meditating under one. From Pakistan, all across India, to Myanmar, it remains an everyday reminder of life's spiritual side. Shrines are built under them, and "to visit the peepal tree" is another way of saying you are going to pray. With a healthy lifespan of up to 1,500 years, the peepal is a good example of the comfort and strength we can all draw from a little bit of positive belief.

Index

Acai palm
p.48

African Acacia
p.45

Alder
p.24

American
beech *p.14*

Ash
p.85

Aspen
p.11

Bald cypress
p.83

Balsam fir
p.51

Banksia
p.89

Banyan
p.54

Baobab
p.37

Beech
p.66, p.98

Blackthorn
p.19

Black tulepo
p.108

Black walnut
p.27

Chestnut
p.30

Chinese
pistache *p.71*

Cook pine
p.117

Cork oak
p.106

Corsican
pine *p.62*

Cottonwood
p.75

Dahurian
larch *p.46*

Douglas
fir *p.72*

Dragon
blood *p.61*

Elm
p.13

European
box *p.78*

Giant sequoia
p.68

Gingko
p.77

Guarea
p.58

Gutta-
percha *p.57*

Hawthorn
p.96

Hazel
p.118

Holly
p.38

Hornbeam
p.16

Japanese
maple *p.6*

Jarrah
p.122

Juniper
p.113

Kauri
p.86

Lilac
p.121

London
plane *p.33*

Mangrove
p.29

Mountain
hemlock *p.22*

Neem
p.111

Oak
p.90

Olive
p.41

Peepal
p.125

Red cedar
p.103

Rowan
p.95

Scots pine
p.92

Sève bleue
p.53

Sierra palm
p.101

Silver birch
p.114

Silver fir
p.34

Sugar maple
p.81

Sycamore
p.105

White
poplar *p.43*

Willow
p.20

Yew
p.9

Yoshino
cherry *p.65*